THE ROSARY
for Little Ones

WRITTEN BY KIMBERLY FRIES

www.mylittlenazareth.com

First Edition: September 2019

Cover by Sue Kouma Johnson

ISBN-13: 9781693438059

This book is dedicated to my daughters,
Maria Rose and Lily Marie.
May you always stay close to Mary.

Every time people say the Rosary devoutly they place a crown of one hundred and fifty-three white roses and sixteen red roses upon the heads of Jesus and Mary.
- St. Louis De Montfort

My Dear Little Ones,

I wonder: Have you ever heard of the great queen with a marvelous garden? The queen's name is Mary, otherwise most lovingly called, Our Lady, and her garden is known even in the most far-off and distant places. Her beautiful, blossoming roses and sweet, fragrant lilies are really quite famous and well-spoken of.

However, the most enchanting part of her garden is not the flowers, but the most spectacular mysteries that lie inside.

I wonder, would you like to visit this most beloved place? You may want to find your rosary or perhaps follow along on the next page. Are you ready? Now find the crucifix, for this is the key to the most magnificent garden, little one, and make the sign of the cross.

You have entered Our Lady's garden.

Rosary Prayers

Make the Sign of the Cross. In the name of the Father, and of the Son, and of the Holy Spirit. Amen.

Pray once: I believe in God, the Father Almighty, creator of heaven and earth; and in Jesus Christ, His only Son, our Lord, who was conceived by the Holy Spirit, born of the Virgin Mary, suffered under Pontius Pilate, was crucified, died, and was buried. He descended into hell; on the third day He rose again from the dead. He ascended into heaven, and is seated at the right hand of God the Father Almighty; from there he will come to judge the living and the dead. I believe in the Holy Spirit, the holy catholic Church, the communion of saints, the forgiveness of sins, the resurrection of the body, and life everlasting. Amen.

Pray once: Our Father, Who art in heaven, hallowed be Thy name; Thy kingdom come; Thy will be done on earth as it is in heaven. Give us this day our daily bread; and forgive us our trespasses as we forgive those who trespass against us; and lead us not into temptation, but deliver us from evil. Amen.

Pray three times for an increase in Faith, Hope, and Love: Hail Mary, full of grace, the Lord is with thee. Blessed art thou amongst women, and blessed is the fruit of thy womb, Jesus. Holy Mary, Mother of God, pray for us sinners, now and at the hour of our death, Amen.

Pray once: Glory be to the Father, and to the Son, and to the Holy Spirit; as it was in the beginning, is now, and ever shall be, world without end. Amen.

Pray once on each big bead: Our Father, Who art in heaven, hallowed be Thy name; Thy kingdom come; Thy will be done on earth as it is in heaven. Give us this day our daily bread; and forgive us our trespasses as we forgive those who trespass against us; and lead us not into temptation, but deliver us from evil. Amen.

Pray once on each small bead: Hail Mary, full of grace, the Lord is with thee. Blessed art thou amongst women, and blessed is the fruit of thy womb, Jesus. Holy Mary, Mother of God, pray for us sinners, now and at the hour of our death. Amen.

Pray once on each big bead: Glory be to the Father, and to the Son, and to the Holy Spirit; as it was in the beginning, is now, and ever shall be, world without end. Amen.

Pray once on each big bead: O my Jesus, forgive us our sins, save us from the fires of hell; lead all souls to Heaven, especially those in most need of thy mercy.

THE JOYFUL
MYSTERIES

THE ANNUNCIATION

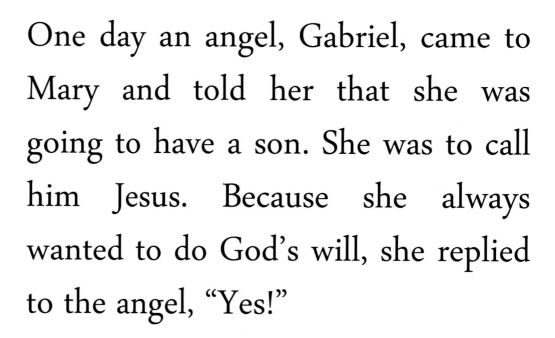

One day an angel, Gabriel, came to Mary and told her that she was going to have a son. She was to call him Jesus. Because she always wanted to do God's will, she replied to the angel, "Yes!"

Jesus, help me always to say "Yes!" to God and follow His commandments.

THE VISITATION

When Jesus was in Mary's womb, she decided to visit her cousin, Elizabeth. As Mary arrived, Elizabeth knew that Jesus was with Mary because the baby in Elizabeth's womb leapt with joy!

Jesus, help me to be really excited about knowing and loving you!

THE NATIVITY

When the time had finally arrived for Jesus to be born, Joseph and Mary were very happy. They knew Jesus was very special. He was just a little baby, innocent and precious. Mary finally could see and hold her son in her arms.

Jesus, you are very precious to me.

THE PRESENTATION

After Jesus was born, Mary and Joseph took Jesus to the temple to be presented to God. At the Temple there was a holy prophet named Simeon. Simeon told Mary that Jesus was going to suffer and that she would suffer with her son.

Dear Jesus, help me to offer up all of my problems and worries to God.

FINDING JESUS IN THE TEMPLE

When Jesus was a child, Joseph and Mary had lost Jesus for three days. Mary and Joseph were very worried about Jesus. Finally, Mary and Joseph found Jesus in the Temple, his Father's house, speaking with the teachers.

Dear Jesus, help me to remember that you are right beside me, even though I cannot see you.

THE LUMINOUS
MYSTERIES

Baptism of Jesus

When Jesus got older, he was baptized in the Jordan River by his cousin, John. As Jesus was baptized, the heavens opened and the Holy Spirit came upon Jesus. A voice from heaven said, "This is my Son, with whom I am well pleased."

Dear Jesus, help me to remember that the Father in heaven loves me so much.

WEDDING AT CANA

The very first miracle of Jesus was done at a wedding in Cana. There was no wine left to drink, so Mary told Jesus about the problem. Jesus told the servers to fill up stone jars with water, but when they poured it out, the water was changed into wine.

Dear Jesus, help me to trust that you and Mary will always take care of me.

PROCLAMATION OF THE KINGDOM OF GOD

Jesus healed many people and taught about the love that the Father has for us. He taught and preached to many people about the coming of his kingdom. Then he sent out his apostles to preach.

Jesus, show me how to tell others about you and your kingdom!

THE TRANSFIGURATION

One day Jesus took Peter, James, and John up a tall mountain. Jesus' clothes became dazzling white and he glowed. He showed how glorious he really is!

Jesus, I want to be transformed just like you! Please help me to be holy!

INSTITUTION OF THE EUCHARIST

On the night before he died, Jesus ate the Last Supper with his apostles. This is when he gave us the Eucharist. He changed bread into his Body and wine into his Blood. He told us to eat his Body and drink his Blood so that we can live forever.

Dear Jesus, thank you so much for giving us your Body and Blood at Mass!

THE SORROWFUL
MYSTERIES

AGONY IN THE GARDEN

After the last supper, Jesus went to a garden to pray. Three of the apostles came with him to the garden, but they all fell asleep. Jesus knew that he would suffer and die the next day. He prayed to his Father. Then the soldiers came to take him away.

Jesus, I am so sad that you were alone. I want to pray more, so I can be with you.

Scourging at the Pillar

After Jesus saw the Roman king Pilate, the soldiers were very mean to Jesus. They tied him up and hit him over and over again.

Jesus, I am so sorry that you had to suffer so much.

CROWNING WITH THORNS

Next soldiers put a crown of thorns on Jesus' head and made fun of him. They laughed at him because they didn't think he was really a king.

Jesus, you are my King! I want to give you a beautiful, shining crown!

CARRYING OF THE CROSS

Jesus carried his cross a long way. He fell three times while carrying his cross. He saw Mary sometimes, which gave him a lot of comfort. A man named Simon helped him carry his cross, too.

Jesus, I want to help others when they are having a hard time.

THE CRUCIFIXION

The soldiers nailed Jesus' hands and feet to the cross. He told his apostle John that Mary was going to be his mother now, and the mother to all of us. Jesus then died.

Jesus, thank you for offering your life for me by dying on the cross.

THE GLORIOUS MYSTERIES

THE RESURRECTION

On Easter Sunday Jesus rose from the dead. When the women saw that the stone was rolled away from his tomb, an angel appeared and said that Jesus had risen! Then they saw Jesus, who said to go tell his apostles.

Jesus, I believe that you rose from the dead!

THE ASCENSION

After forty days of being on earth, Jesus told his disciples to go out and baptize others and teach them about God. Then, the gates of heaven opened and Jesus ascended into heaven. But he promised to be with us until the end of time.

Jesus, I know that you are always with me, even though I can't see you.

DESCENT OF THE HOLY SPIRIT

Ten days later, the Holy Spirit came to the apostles in the upper room. Wind came into the room and tongues of fire appeared above the apostles' head. They were filled with the Holy Spirit and unafraid to tell everyone about Jesus.

Jesus, let me receive the Holy Spirit so I can share all about you!

The Assumption

After Mary died and was laid in a tomb, God took her body to heaven. She finally got to be with her son, Jesus, in heaven.

Jesus, how much you must have loved bringing Mary to heaven with you!

THE CORONATION

Mary was then crowned Queen of Heaven and Earth by Jesus. She is the queen of all of the angels and saints and our special Heavenly Mother, too.

Jesus, I cannot wait until I can go to heaven to see you, Mary, and all the saints and angels!

Pray once: Hail, holy Queen, mother of mercy, our life, our sweetness, and our hope. To thee do we cry, poor banished children of Eve; to thee do we send up our sighs, mourning and weeping in this valley of tears. Turn then, most gracious advocate, thine eyes of mercy toward us, and after this our exile, show unto us the blessed fruit of thy womb, Jesus. O clement, O loving, O sweet Virgin Mary. Pray for us, O holy Mother of God, that we may be made worthy of the promises of Christ.

Pray once: O God, whose only begotten Son, by His life, death, and resurrection, has purchased for us the rewards of eternal life. Grant, we beseech Thee, that by meditating upon these mysteries of the most holy Rosary of the Blessed Virgin Mary, we may imitate what they contain and obtain what they promise, through the same Christ our Lord. Amen.

Pray once: In the name of the Father, and of the Son, and of the Holy Spirit. Amen.

COLLECT ALL THE
MY LITTLE NAZARETH BOOKS

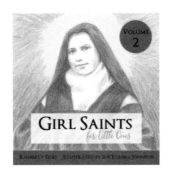
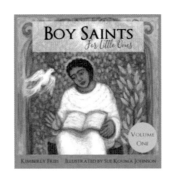

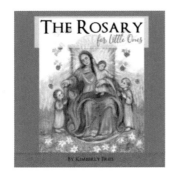
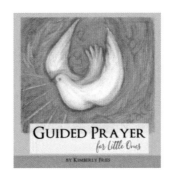

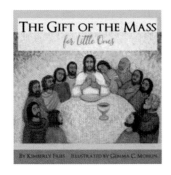

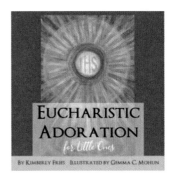

Meet the Author

I'm Kimberly Fries, homeschooling mom and author. I live in South Dakota with my husband and three children. Creating Catholic books to help children develop a personal relationship with God, Mary, and the saints has been such a joy for me. I pray that my books greatly bless your family and assist you in your journey to become saints!

I would love to hear from you!

Please write a review at Amazon.com.

Want to be the first to know about my new releases?
Follow me on Facebook, Instagram, Youtube, and my blog!
www.mylittlenazareth.com

Interested in getting wholesale prices?
E-mail me at mylittlenazareth@gmail.com